Praise for *Dancing with Monsters*

"This exciting, quick-moving fable has all the important lessons of a 300-page textbook many leadership and business programs would assign to their students. Since the lessons are relayed in story form, the reader is connected, emotionally invested, and empathizing with the characters—which all means the lessons are more memorable than a traditional business book. But Dr. Todd Dewett doesn't stop with the fable. He closes with practical advice leaders in all industries and levels need to take seriously and leaves us with helpful reflection questions to guide our discussions on this book, unpack the lessons, and plan out our future leadership solutions. I am confident this book will help many leaders and future leaders dance with monsters with eagerness and greater success throughout their careers."

—Chrissy Roth-Francis, Ed.D., Director of Talent Development, LinkedIn

"Todd is an authentic storyteller! I started reading it and couldn't stop! He talks about the fundamentals of leadership in the most engaging way! I can see *Dancing with Monsters* becoming THE business book for workshops

and coaching interventions and that's how
I am personally intending to use it. He talks
about the psychology of fear without becoming
psychological and how it can be a leader's
Achilles Heel. A definite MUST-=READ!"
—Dr. Maria Katsarou-Makin, Founder,
Leadership Psychology Institute

"Our unseen and unacknowledged fears
arguably have a more profound impact on
our leadership effectiveness than any other
element. This book is an incredibly fun yet
deeply insightful journey into understanding
these dynamics, along with a very pragmatic
point of view on how to move forward from
where you are. Todd's ability to cut through
the surface and get to the root of leadership
derailers comes through in his writing here as
well as he does in his live seminars."
—Bob Kalka, Global Vice-President,
IBM Security, and Author of *The*
Emotionally Authentic Christian

"Todd's written a playful, powerful book on
how we can address our fears to embrace
authentic leadership. Find me a leader who
doesn't have fears and self-doubt—this
book tackles them head on. It's full of real-
world tips, including my favorite 'If you

want a high-performing team, it's a war for chemistry, not talent' (aka, no jerks). I appreciated his call to action on realizing the power of now and opening up to share your own vulnerabilities in order to bond with and motivate your team—and accomplish more together. Great read!"

—Jolie Miller, Director of Content, Business & Creative at LinkedIn Learning

"Through an engaging story, Todd shares a practical framework for personal and professional growth. The value of candor, collaboration, courage, and commitment come to life. He reminds us that great progress can be made when we embrace our imperfections, face our fears, and try new things. As Todd shares, 'Take a step. Get the scare. Grow. Win.' This book is a must for leaders at all levels! The advice and tips on overcoming your fears and using them as a springboard for growth, the value of continuous learning, and thoughtful communication are all foundational to building strong relationships and increasing your confidence as you lead yourself, lead others, and lead the business."

—Victoria Di Santo, Director, Organizational Development & Effectiveness, Brother International Corporation

"*Dancing with Monsters* provokes deep thought and reflections around some key questions: 'What do you want?', 'Why do you want it?', and 'What are you afraid of?'. I would recommend any seasoned, new, or aspiring leader read this book and invite answers to those questions. We're all afraid of something and we all have hopes and dreams in the clouds."

—Charles Newnam, Strategy Principal Director, Accenture

"Success begins with your story. And when you change your story, you change your results. Join this journey of discovery about how the monsters we encounter along the road to success can be conquered in a simple sentence. Thanks to Dr. Dewett, your once-upon-a-time starts now."

—Karen Mangia, *Wall Street Journal* Bestselling Author & Vice President Customer & Market Insights, Salesforce

DANCING
WITH
MONSTERS

Also by Todd Dewett, PhD

Show Your Ink
Live Hard
The Ten Delusions
The Little Black Book of Leadership

DANCING

WITH

MONSTERS

A Tale About Leadership,

Success, and Overcoming Fears

TODD DEWETT, PHD

Matt Holt Books
An Imprint of BenBella Books, Inc.
Dallas, TX

Dancing with Monsters copyright © 2023 by TVA Inc.

Matt Holt is an imprint of BenBella Books, Inc.
10440 N. Central Expressway
Suite 800
Dallas, TX 75231
benbellabooks.com
Send feedback to feedback@benbellabooks.com

BenBella and *Matt Holt* are federally registered trademarks.

Printed in the United States of America
10 9 8 7 6 5 4 3 2 1

Library of Congress Control Number: 2022040504
ISBN 9781637743270 (hardcover)
ISBN 9781637743287 (electronic)

Copyediting by Michael Fedison
Proofreading by Jenny Rosen and Ariel Fagiola
Text design and composition by PerfecType
Cover design by Brigid Pearson
Illustrations by Paul Weiner
Printed by Lake Book Manufacturing

Special discounts for bulk sales are available. Please contact bulkorders@benbellabooks.com.

To my sons, Paxon and Parker—you are my favorite monsters. Your kindness, humor, and hard work inspire me to keep trying, creating, and moving forward. The world is better for having you two in it! Love you.

CONTENTS

INTRODUCTION

We all have monsters in our lives, fears that slow us down and sometimes completely derail us. These might include a fear of failure, fear of not being smart enough, fear of not being accepted and valued, or a fear that our imperfections define us as unworthy. These ideas infect our personal and professional lives. They stop us from growing and achieving.

Similarly, many leaders at work perceive imperfections in their team members. They see conflict, personality differences, motivational issues, and performance problems. Sometimes the employees seem like monsters. It's an overly negative focus on these issues that stops leaders from harnessing the team's true power.

Overcoming your fears and leading others are similar in some ways. They both require us to view ourselves with honesty and to view others with empathy and respect. We have to see the beauty in the monster. That's when you start to build the confidence needed to face the normal risks associated with learning and success. So don't fear the challenges and imperfections, whether in yourself or others. It's time to stop denying, avoiding, or denigrating them. It's time to go dancing with monsters.

PART
1

The Dilemma

Maria and Noah followed their typical Sunday morning routine. They got up, dressed without trying to impress, and headed to their favorite local coffee shop. They could make wonderful coffee at home, but there was something special about walking into their local spot, smelling the aroma of freshly brewed coffee, and seeing a few familiar faces. When it wasn't crowded, they often chose to stay and lounge for a while. This particular morning was a chilly affair in October, just a few weeks before Halloween.

"I guess the cold is keeping people at home," Maria said as they waited on their order.

"Good. I brought a book and my laptop. Want to have a seat?" Noah asked.

She nodded.

The pair grabbed their drinks when they were ready and sank into two overstuffed armchairs.

"Have you thought any more about what you want to be for Halloween?" Maria asked.

"Yes. Happy," Noah replied. He noticed the look of concern on Maria's face. "Sorry. That comment has nothing to do with you. I've just been thinking about work."

"What's wrong at work?" Maria asked.

"There's something I haven't told you," Noah replied.

Maria looked a little worried.

"I've been offered a promotion," he said.

"That's amazing! It's what you wanted. It's what we wanted," Maria said and then noticed that his face did not look happy. "What's wrong?"

"There's something else I didn't tell you," Noah continued. "It's a manager role for a team that has been underperforming. People talk about them. They want to make me captain of a sinking ship. There's more—there are eight people on the team and one of them is Miles."

"Oh! Icky. I remember that guy. First of all," she said, "congratulations. This is a huge deal—your first promotion into a leadership role. When did they approach you?"

"They told me Wednesday," Noah replied.

She smacked his arm lightly. "I'm your wife and you've been sitting on this since Wednesday?"

"That was a mistake. You know I normally don't do that. I'm sorry. There's just something about this decision that's bugging me," he said.

"When do you have to make your decision?" Maria asked.

"They want to know tomorrow," he replied.

She smacked his arm again. Maria couldn't believe he was only telling her now. "Okay, let's talk this through, starting with Miles."

"You know that Miles and I have a history, but you don't know all of it," he said.

"I only know that you went to high school and college at the same schools and that he's full of himself," she replied.

"There's more," Noah began. "In high school, he was the popular kid. He started on the varsity basketball team while I came off the bench. In college, he walked on the team and played for two years. I tried to walk on and didn't make it. He joined a big fraternity. I kind of wanted to but couldn't afford it. The first girl I had a crush on, he dated, and yes, he knew how I felt about her."

"Yikes," Maria said.

"It gets worse. We got in a fight once at a party. There was drinking involved. He was really rude to a girl. I said something.

Shoving turned into punching. We both landed a few shots and then, thankfully, calmed down and blew it off."

Maria's eyes bulged in surprise.

"He finished with a slightly better GPA than mine and then landed the best job of anyone in our whole accounting program that year. Two years later, our firm lured him over."

"He's a senior associate like you?" Maria asked.

"Yup, we're on the same level, but in different groups. Truthfully, he's a better accountant—clients love him—and I'm a better people person," Noah replied.

"I've met the guy . . . Why do they love him so much?" Maria asked.

8

"He's very bright and solves their problems. They're happy to overlook his personality," he said. "And I have it on good authority that he went after the promotion too. I hope it doesn't get weird. Miles is not well liked at work. It's a classic case of a company putting up with a jerk because he's highly talented."

"And you remember what our favorite professor said about that, right?" Maria asked.

Noah nodded. "No amount of talent justifies consistent jerk behavior, because if high performance is your goal, it's a war for chemistry, not talent."

"That's right, and I have to say, your description does not surprise me based on my few interactions with Miles," Maria said. Her eyes darted away as a thought hit her. "Wait! Wait a second. Now this all makes sense. He's also your dad's best friend's son."

"Bingo. You remembered," Noah said. "Somehow I fell for accounting and followed Dad's path into a role at one of the big firms. He couldn't be prouder and can't wait for me to start climbing the leadership ranks. He won't admit it, but I think he also wants me to advance faster than Miles."

"And you're going to," Maria said with a cocky smirk.

"The problem is that I can't accept the way Miles behaves. Yelling, belittling, and so on. He gets away with a lot because, well, I assume because he's super talented and the senior team doesn't really understand how bad the problem is."

"So, what do you want to do?" Maria asked.

"I've actually been thinking about letting him go," Noah responded.

Again, Maria flashed a look of surprise. "That's harsh. How would the brass react if he's such a superstar? Plus, don't you want to give him a chance to adjust to you? Maybe he'll get the picture and shape up."

Noah thought for a moment. "Well, letting him go would definitely cause a problem. You're right. As usual," he said.

"So, you're going to deal with him and accept the promotion?" she asked.

"That's why I was scared to talk to you. I'm not sure. I know I'm ready to lead. If I say yes and I'm successful, my dad will be thrilled. However, if at some point, I have to reprimand or fire Miles, Dad's buddy will find out and it will be weird between them. And if I do some type of intervention with Miles, there's no telling what type of damage he might try to do to me. On the other hand, if I choose to pass on this specific promotion, it will be a long time before they offer me another," Noah said.

"It does sound like a challenge," Maria said.

"And on top of the Miles issue," Noah continued, "the team apparently has some serious issues. On nearly every metric, they underperform compared to other groups. They are actually the second group Miles has been with. It didn't take long for everyone to figure out how tough it is to deal with him once he arrived. So, blinded by his talent, they decided to keep him and put him in the one questionable group in the firm. Overall, he actually makes their stats look a little better. I know a couple of his teammates. They told me people basically leave him alone and only interact with him when completely necessary. It's not a happy team. I don't know. I feel like I'm being set up to fail."

"Or maybe they believe you're the only one who can save the sinking ship. And when you address Miles and turn the team around, it won't just be a win, it will be a giant win. One that puts you on the map—know what I mean?" Maria said.

"You do have a point," Noah replied.

"I have to ask—is there anything else you want to tell me?" Maria asked sarcastically.

"No," he replied and smiled. "I know where I fit. I enjoy the firm and I have some good ideas for turning the team around. But . . . I don't know if this role is worth the risk.

You only get to be a new leader once, you know?"

"Hmm. Your situation reminds me of the monster story that same professor made us read. Do you remember it?" she asked.

"Maybe some of it?" Noah replied.

"Scooch closer," Maria said as she took out her tablet and tapped the screen a few times. "I've still got a copy in my library."

Noah smiled and moved closer so they could read it together.

PART
2

Dancing with
Monsters

The
Precipice

Once upon a time in Monster Land a vampire named Joe was feeling sorry for himself. He sat in the shade under a large tree in front of the Monster Central building. It was early before his shift started and he wasn't looking forward to it. He wasn't sure why, but he had begun to lose his once mighty confidence in his ability to scare.

"But at least I look good," he thought.

His dark hair was slicked back just so. A dark suit, a dark cape, and dark sunglasses completed his classic look. It was the Ray-Bans in particular that had gotten him in a bit of hot water. Monster accessories were generally frowned upon as distractions from a monster's true essence. It was believed they would interfere with the ability to scare children—the ultimate goal of every monster.

Cool looks aside, Joe felt he was slipping into depression. He'd lost his passion for creating fright. Good scares were hard to come by lately. Joe came from a long line of successful vampires. His father ran the most successful vampire training academy in Monster Land. The plan was for Joe to prove himself in the field and then assume a leadership role in the family business. Now he risked returning to the family in disgrace—a vampire who couldn't scare.

Joe felt small—because he was. Scares were the magic elixir that made monsters grow. The more you scare, the bigger you get. He watched a long line of successful monsters stroll by confidently. They looked enormous. He felt jealous and resentful. Thanks to his family's success, he had a sense of entitlement, and he knew it. He hadn't earned the right to grow, but he still wanted to be bigger.

From behind him came a sound he knew well—that of a rapidly approaching broom. The witch in control of the broom was looking for Joe. She spotted him and glided down to the bench where he sat, leaving a long line of smoke behind her.

"Joe Vampire. We need to talk," the administrator said, glancing around to gauge their privacy.

It hurt Joe to look at her. When he'd started in the field, the witch was so kind, almost kissing up to him. Now, she looked down her long pointy nose with disdain. Joe had no idea what she wanted.

"You're not to report to work today. You have a new assignment," she said.

She motioned for him to follow and walked with him into Monster Central. They quickly entered a series of back rooms. She waved him into one particular conference room.

"That's better," she said. She closed the door, sat down, and removed her huge floppy black hat. When Joe was also seated, she took a deep breath and began, "Joe, the committee has made a decision."

Joe immediately knew he was in trouble. The committee ran everything in Monster Land, and they never interacted with field personnel. That was the job of the administrators like the witch.

"We've given you as much feedback and time as we can. The committee wants you to know you're in jeopardy of losing your monster status. Monsters scare, Joe—that's the simple truth. You've shown great promise in the past but have slipped into a long period of, well, questionable performance."

Joe sat quietly, worried about what she might say next.

"Are you listening?" she asked. "I can't see your eyes through those ridiculous glasses."

Joe refrained from removing his sunglasses. "I'm listening," he replied.

"Joe, we respect where you came from—in fact, we like you. But this is your last chance. Just so you know, our protocols required us to inform your family of your status."

"You told my family I'm about to be kicked out? My father too?" he asked in a mild panic.

She nodded. "It's protocol. However, we've devised one last project for you. We are hopeful it gives you the boost you need to get back on the path to becoming one of our premier monsters."

Joe knew that anything would be better than returning home having failed his family. "Okay. What do you want me to do?"

"We want you to step up and lead a group," the witch replied. "This is a special group, Joe. It's a group of monsters who are having great difficulty being monsters. More difficulty than you've experienced. In fact, each of them has yet to produce even one scare."

"You're serious?" Joe asked.

"Normally, they would have just washed out by now, but we think working with you just might be what they need—and what you need," she said and paused to watch his reaction.

Joe did not like the idea of having to prove himself. He truly disliked the idea of working with rejects. He also knew that he had no choice. He could not disappoint his father. He could not return home a failure.

"I'm in. When do I start?" he said with fake enthusiasm.

"Right now," the witch replied. "Stay here. I'll be right back."

Joe sat nervously and waited. "How bad could it be?" he thought.

Moments later, the door opened. The witch walked in followed by a girl wearing cat ears, a ghost wearing a silly Halloween ghost mask, a scrawny, almost sick-looking mummy, and a very off-balance zombie who walked with the help of a crutch.

"You're kidding me, right?" Joe thought.

A Broken
Team

When they were all seated around the table, the witch asked them to introduce themselves and gestured to the girl with the cat ears.

"Hi. I'm Wolfy," she said in a tiny voice.

"So, you're a werewolf?" Joe thought.

"I'm Sheets," the ghost with the mask offered with an equally meek voice.

Joe wondered if this was a prank.

The loose collection of bandages went next. "Hello, everyone. I'm Mum."

Joe glanced at the witch to see if she was laughing.

The weary-looking zombie nodded and spoke up. "I'm Z," he said in a gravelly voice. "I like your cape."

Joe gave Z a weak smile and then glanced around the table. It was the least scary group of misfit monsters he'd ever seen.

"Joe, they've been briefed on your background," the witch continued. "My job is to tell you about the task before you. You're all being put on notice. You must learn to scare children, or you will be stripped of your monster status forever and banned from field activities. Joe is going to lead the effort. Your goal is to collectively create one hundred scares before the next monster's ball.

"One hundred?" Mum asked. "Isn't the next ball tonight?"

All of their faces registered shock and disbelief—including Joe's.

The witch nodded affirmatively and stood up. "The committee didn't have to give you this opportunity. To be honest, it will be tough, but I'm pulling for you. One hundred scares by tonight. How you do it is up to you. Any questions?" She didn't pause before continuing, "Great. The clock is ticking. Get busy. Good luck."

The witch put on her huge floppy black hat, jumped on her broom, and zoomed out the door.

The group sat quietly. Some looked at Joe; others stared at the table.

Joe tried to remember his training from long ago. His grandfather founded the family's vampire training academy, and leadership was a core part of the curriculum. He drew a blank trying to recall specifics. He did, however, recall a heavy focus on communication.

"Well, all right, then. You all look quite surprised. Me too," Joe said. "It appears we have a lot of work to do, but maybe we can just start by getting to know each other for a minute. I'd like to know a little about you and how you ended up with us today. Who wants to start?"

Silence persisted for a few moments until Wolfy finally spoke up. "I've been having a lot of trouble transforming. I'm a werewolf—at least I think I am. I've been meaning to find help—you know, a coach or something—but I just keep putting it off. No scares. So here I am."

"For me," Sheets said, "it's about trying new things—I hate that.

I actually did talk to a few more experienced friends, and they all told me to do a bunch of new things, including taking off my mask. I have a baby face underneath. It's just not scary."

Everyone stared at the plastic ghost-faced mask covering his small face.

"But I love my mask. It makes me feel comfortable, even if it's not scary," he finished.

"I know a thing or two about not being scary," Mum offered.

The group looked at her but could barely see her bandaged face because it was obscured by the hood of her ginormous gray hoodie.

"Everyone in my family kept waiting for me to grow, but it never happened," she continued. "I never grew into my wrappings, so they just look droopy and strange—definitely not scary."

"I think I could have been scary," Z said. "Trouble is, the monster administration created a rigged system. You can't get ahead unless you know the right people. Plus, if you get hurt," he said as he lifted his rotting leg to show everyone his missing right foot, "they don't give you any help. I had to find this crutch on my own! I'm telling you. I could've been scary."

During another moment of silence, they all began to stare at Joe. They assumed Joe was an administrator, too, there to educate and train them to be scary. They examined him, judged him to be confident and cool, and hoped he would be the coach to guide them through this horrible dilemma.

"Well," Joe thought, "it's a rough bunch, but at least they seem ready to open up and talk about it. That's something."

"Everyone, if you're going to get better at scaring kids, you have to start with thinking about the root cause of what's been stopping you. I want to hear from each of you. What is it you really fear?" Joe asked, surprised at how leader-like his question sounded.

"I'll go. I'm afraid of never transforming and never scaring. I guess that's a basic fear of failure?" Wolfy said quietly. She adjusted her ears and continued, "My parents are fearsome—same with my siblings. I'm the runt of the litter and feel like a disappointment. I'm just defective. One hundred scares is crazy, but at least we've got some time, so there's no need to stress out, right?" It was obvious to all that Wolfy was definitely stressing out. "Maybe we should just stay here and plan something, or let Joe train us first?"

"What I fear is that no amount of training will fix me," Mum said from beneath her hoodie. "It's just the reality. I'm frail and weak. Most people think I'm just a funny-looking kid wearing adult clothing that doesn't fit."

"Don't say that," Joe said. "Who knows what you're capable of. You can't know until you try." He wished he meant what he said. "What about you?" He pointed to Sheets.

"I'm not sure what to say. I just like keeping to myself. I don't really like scaring kids. What did they ever do to us anyway? Besides, to learn to scare probably means to change something I'm doing, so I'm not thrilled about it. At this late hour, does it really matter?" Sheets seemed totally without hope.

"It's not your fault," Z chimed in. "You were born the way you were. I was born the way I am. Well, I had two feet back then. Now I'm just broken." He looked at Joe and then lowered his head. "The system is biased too. So, I fear that I'm too broken to scare. Too broken to hold almost any role in Monster Land."

Joe listened as they continued speaking poorly of themselves. He'd been feeling sorry for himself earlier, but this was insane! He'd never seen a more weak-minded, sorry-looking, blame-filled, low-confidence group in his life. If he wasn't being forced to take on this task, he'd never be caught dead hanging around this crew. Joe felt defeated before they had even begun.

Impossible
Dreams

J oe gave himself a little pep talk. "You can do this. It's a means to an end. They can't be as bad as they seem. Get it done and move on!" he thought.

"Okay, everyone, follow me. Concerns aside, we've got work to do. Time is short, so let's do this!" Joe exclaimed with obviously contrived enthusiasm.

Wolfy sat still and just cringed. She really wanted to go take a nap and just forget about the whole thing. "One hundred scares? Impossible," she thought.

Mum complied and stood up, briefly tripping over her loose bandages.

Z followed suit, mumbling under his breath, "This just ain't fair."

Sheets rose slowly, petrified that Joe was about to make him try to be scary.

Wolfy finally got up as well.

Joe guided the group out of the office and through the main corridor in Monster Central. They passed hordes of larger monsters as they walked. Everyone in the group stared up at them, some with admiration, others with animosity.

"Is he taking us where I think he's taking us?" Wolfy asked Sheets.

"I think so. The only thing up that way is the wall," he replied. "I was hoping for some training facility or something."

"Nope," Mum said. "We're jumping right into the fire. Seriously, can we

46

just skip this part and turn in our monster badges?"

"Slow down!" Z yelled. "You are all walking too fast. I can't scare anyone if I'm in pain!"

Mum stopped to wait on Z as Joe arrived at the huge double doors.

"We're here. I hate this place," Wolfy whispered to Sheets.

"It scares me," Sheets replied.

"We've got this. Follow me," Joe said with more fake enthusiasm. He opened the grand double doors to reveal a massive wall of clouds.

The group followed Joe past several crowded areas full of monsters entering clouds and tormenting children. Finally, they found an area big enough for all of them to participate.

Looking up at the vast wall, Joe hoped he wasn't wasting his time. Each cloud was a gateway to a child's bedroom. "So many clouds. So many kids. Surely, we can scare a few of them," he thought.

Joe motioned for everyone to gather around him in a close huddle. "You are monsters," he began. "Scaring is what you were built to do. Sure, you've experienced a few bumps along the way—so what? It's time to pick yourselves up, dust yourselves off, and start scaring!"

The group looked at him, deeply concerned.

Joe ignored their gloom and continued the act. He had to—they were his lifeline. He had to make this work or return home a loser.

"Sheets! You're going first. Let me see . . . That looks like a good one," Joe said and pointed to a cloud. "Get in there, Sheets, and show that kid who's boss!"

"But I—" Sheets began to say.

"No *buts*! This starts with you. That's an order," Joe replied.

Sheets walked reluctantly up to the cloud and paused.

After everything the group had discussed, Joe assumed he would take off his mask.

Sheets took a deep breath. He walked slowly through the cloud as the others watched, his mask still in place over his face. Sheets quickly found himself inside a closet. The door was cracked. He peered out and saw exactly what he expected—a child dozing off and beginning to enter dreamland. Sheets exhaled, opened the door, and approached the child.

"Boo! Booooo!" Sheets used his standard approach. He just stood there next to the bed and kept saying, "Boo!"

The young boy shook off the cobwebs and sat up. "Dad? Is that you?"

"Boo!" Sheets tried once more.

"Seriously? Not scary. Wait, is that you, Steven?"

Sheets realized the child thought he was his brother dressed like a ghost.

"That's a stupid mask, you big dummy!" the child yelled and flung a pillow at Sheets's face.

Sheets's mask was badly askew after a direct hit from the pillow. When he saw the boy beginning to get out of bed, he hurried back to the closet.

When he emerged from the cloud, the group clearly felt bad for him.

"Not your fault, young man," Z said. "You could have never known that kid was violent."

"There's always next time, Sheets," Mum offered.

Joe quickly brushed off the setback and turned to Wolfy. He realized he'd bossed Sheets around a bit, so he decided to be nice—even if it was an act.

"Wolfy, you can get us moving in the right direction. I believe in you.

Look at those ears—you're fierce!"
Joe went a bit over the top.

"Really?" Wolfy responded.

"Super fierce!" Joe replied, hoping
they all believed him—especially
Wolfy. "Okay." He motioned to the
wall of clouds. "Take a look at these
options and pick the one you feel is
right for you."

Wolfy pondered a group of about
ten clouds, peeked inside a few, and
finally chose one. She glanced at Joe
and the group.

Mum nodded and showed her
fingers crossed for good luck.

Joe smiled a beautiful fake smile.

Z offered a fake smile of his own.
"Are we sure this girl is a monster?"
he whispered to Sheets.

Sheets didn't reply, nor could he bring himself to watch as Wolfy walked into the cloud.

Wolfy found herself under a child's bed in the dark. She took a deep breath and shimmied her way out. When she stood up, she saw a little girl who was already fast asleep. "It's easy," she told herself. "Wake the kid up, transform, be scary."

She carefully reached down and poked the little girl on the shoulder a few times until she woke up. Wolfy clenched her fists, grimaced, closed her eyes, and tried to change. Nothing. She tried again. Nothing.

The little girl screamed, "Mommy! Mommy! There's a stranger in my room!" Then the girl revealed her weapon—a lifelike baby doll with a hard, plastic face. She hurled it at Wolfy's head and nearly knocked the cat ears from their perch. When Wolfy heard the steps approaching from outside the child's room, she dove to the floor and rolled under the bed.

Emerging from the cloud, she glared sadly at Joe as if to say, "I thought you said I was fierce." She walked a safe distance away from the group and sulked.

Joe wasn't sure if she was crying, but he couldn't afford to care. They had to learn to scare, and they had to learn now!

"All right, Z, I need you to show us how it's done. You're the most experienced fiend in the group,"

Joe said while scanning the wall,
looking for an easy mark to scare.
He found one and finally looked at
Z. "Remember, we have to do this or
else. Careers are at stake. We are
all counting on you to save us!" He
wondered if Z would drop his crutch.

Somehow Z felt moved by Joe's
crazy pitch, or at least by the
situation. "Okay, cape-man," he
said. Z kept the crutch and hobbled
hesitantly into the cloud. On
the other side, he found himself
standing in a dark corner of a child's
room. The boy in bed looked tiny and
fragile. "This can't be that hard,"
Z figured.

Z moved forward just a bit and
began to make scratchy noises

and offered the beginning of a zombie moan.

The child started to wake up. He looked timidly toward the dark corner of the room.

Z knew this was it. Time to make the magic happen! He reached out menacingly with his free hand and stepped out of the dark into the soft light created by the boy's night-light. His crutch immediately landed on the bed of a tiny toy truck. Z fell awkwardly to the ground and landed with a painful thud.

The child giggled as he watched Z squirm.

"Rafa!" someone yelled from down the hall.

Z knew it was time to run. He attempted to stand but slipped again. He crawled to the corner, almost forgetting to grab his crutch from the child's floor. He disappeared in the corner as a concerned parent stormed into the room.

Joe helped Z to his feet and brushed him off. "Are you okay?"

Z did not answer. His pride was quite bruised. He shuffled toward Wolfy at the back of the group.

"Listen, it's okay. We are just beginning. We'll figure it out. And"— he turned to face Mum—"I bet that it starts with you."

Mum was frozen in fear, having just watched multiple failures.

"Mum, I do this all the time. I have thousands of scares under my belt. You know why? I'm not scared! We do the scaring. You can do this too! You just have to believe. Now, you might want to—" Joe began to say as Mum started walking numbly toward the closest cloud.

"The sooner I do this, the sooner I can stop trying to be a monster," she thought.

Joe was going to suggest she remove her oversized hoodie, but he was too late.

Mum disappeared into the cloud and came out snugly under the covers next to a small girl. As she thought for a moment about how best to scare the child, she shifted to gain a little room under the heavy covers. She quickly realized she was tangled in a mix of her bandages, her hoodie, and the sheets.

The child sensed the commotion and sat up. She had no idea what was under the covers. She did know that she did not want it there. She kicked furiously and sent Mum falling to the floor in a jumble of bandages and bedsheets.

Mum glanced up and could see the child standing up on the bed. She feared the tot was going to jump on her. She grabbed one of the fallen bedsheets, covered herself, and hastily made her exit. When she was back with the others, she was in a shambles, bandages drooping and dragging everywhere.

Joe didn't know what to say.

Mum walked delicately toward the back near Wolfy, holding her bandages up with both hands.

"I guess that's the end of this," Sheets offered from behind his mask.

"Don't worry, everyone," Z spoke up. "It's not your fault."

Joe wondered if Z's words were directed to him. He sensed a little anger mixed in with their sour mood.

"Too bad we can't go through together like a real team," Wolfy said.

Joe made a mental note.

"To be honest, right now I just want a nap—and some food," Wolfy offered.

Joe turned to look at Wolfy. "We can't wait long, but you're right—we definitely need some lunch. That wasn't a bad effort at all. We'll get on track after lunch for sure. Okay, everyone is on their own for now.

Let's meet back here in exactly
one hour."

It only took a moment for all of
them to walk away, leaving Joe
standing alone in front of the wall.
He looked at the enormous structure
and the innumerable clouds. What
once looked like endless possibilities
now felt like a crushing burden.

Second
Chances

Joe took refuge back in the conference room where he'd first met the group. "Is this how it ends?" he thought. Despair washed over him. Joe closed his eyes behind his shiny Ray-Bans. He thought back to a time when life seemed so full of opportunity. He was a young vampire breezing through his training and initial fieldwork. He quickly became the one to watch in his rookie class.

As the first few years passed, Joe found progress elusive. His family's support and kindness faded. Rubbing elbows every day with witches, ghosts, werewolves, zombies, and every other form of monster became tiresome. His skills did not mature. He wasn't sure he belonged.

Another monster even made fun of him once when they found out how few scares Joe had actually created. That memory made him think about the group he'd been charged with leading. Maybe he didn't want to admit it, but he could relate to them.

Joe looked up and saw his reflection in the glass windows surrounding the conference room. "Maybe I am them," he thought. "They are definitely imperfect, but maybe I am too. Maybe I'm part of the problem. How can I expect them to improve when I can't admit that I'm just as broken? Maybe another try will work if we approach it much differently."

"That's a lot of *maybes*," Joe said out loud and grinned. He took off his glasses and looked at himself again for a long moment. He knew what he had to do.

After lunch, the group arrived at the section of the wall where they had been working. Joe was not there. Instead, they found a sign taped to the wall that read, "Meet me in the conference room—Joe."

As they filed in, Joe noticed the worrisome looks on their faces. He could tell they assumed he was throwing in the towel after watching their abysmal performances earlier in the day.

"Hi. Hello. Welcome back. Everyone take a seat, please," Joe said from his chair at the head of the table.

When everyone settled in, Joe
sat up straight and rolled the dice.
"Based on how I was introduced
to you and how you treated me, I
gathered that you all thought I was
part of the administration, like
the witch."

Heads nodded around the table.

"I'm not. I'd like to start over. If
you don't mind," Joe said.

He paused to look at their
reaction. They seemed curious.

"Hi. My name is Joe," he began.
"I'm a monster just like you. I have
also been put on notice due to
questionable performance. I'm not
entirely sure why they asked me to
lead this project, but I was told that,
like you, if I'm not successful, it's the
end of my monster status too."

He swallowed and continued, "I don't have thousands of scares. That was a lie. It's more like a few hundred."

The group gasped, surprised to hear him speak so plainly.

"As I look back on this morning, I'm pretty sure I was short with you, or maybe condescending or even arrogant. I need to apologize for that. Don't laugh, but the administration once looked at me as an up-and-coming superstar. I don't know if I ever deserved that, but it's true. What I do know is that if I get kicked out, I'll be the black sheep in my family forever. I don't want that. So, I thought I'd come clean with you. You all shared—bravely, I might add—a lot of your fears with me. I

shared none with you, until now,"
Joe said.

He raised his right hand and
removed his sunglasses. His eyes
were closed. He opened them slowly,
revealing two starkly green eyes.

They all gasped again. Looks of
shock dominated the faces around
the table. Mum covered her mouth in
disbelief. Wolfy jerked backward just
a bit. Sheets pulled down his mask
to get a good look. Z simply couldn't
believe what he saw.

All vampires have bright red eyes.
They glow like embers. Joe's eyes
were a piercing green.

They had never seen a vampire
with green eyes. They weren't sure
how to react.

Joe placed his Ray-Bans on top of his head and continued. "Here's what I fear. I fear not being as scary as my father and grandfather. I worry that people will always look at my eyes and judge me before they even know me. I fear not having the guts to be who I want to be before it's too late. Instead of focusing on how I could be a better monster, I always just sneered down my nose at others and expected people to be kind to me. It felt for a time like I was a young superstar, but now I wonder if I was just lucky to be born into a good situation. If I spoke down to you this morning, I'm sincerely sorry."

He noticed Mum wipe her eyes. Wolfy clung to every word he was

saying. Sheets and Z couldn't
look away.

"Wow, maybe I should have gotten
honest a long time ago," Joe thought.

"The truth is we're all imperfect,"
he continued. "That reality is funny,
it's horrible, it's natural, and maybe
it's okay. I did some thinking while
you were gone. I remembered the
time my grandfather—a terribly
successful vampire—singled me out
for leadership training at youth
vamp camp. He tasked me with
leading a group of young trainees
through a forest expedition. I was a
bit nervous since I was the same age
as those I was charged with leading.
My grandfather saw my hesitation
and pulled me aside. He told me that
leading is easy. He said you just have

to respect them, which means don't be a dictator, be straight with them, help them see the glass half full, and don't act—because they'll know. That last bit was his favorite. He believed in authenticity. Then he told me to strive for one small win to kick-start a little momentum, and the rest would take care of itself."

"Is that what happened?" Wolfy asked.

"Oh no. I failed miserably. I got everyone lost, two young vampires were injured, and my grandfather had to lead another expedition just to come find us. It was a total disaster," Joe replied.

"But they sent you out with no real training," Z said, "so that's not really your fault."

"Today, I think I've started to realize that explaining setbacks like that expedition is never really a black-and-white situation. There are many factors to consider, and for that disaster one of them was definitely me. Looking back, I don't think I actually followed any of my grandfather's rules!" Joe said, half laughing.

"More importantly, what I've realized is that if I want to, I can try again. We can try again," Joe said. "So, what do you say?" He stood up, bright green eyes glancing around the table. "Will you work with me and try again?"

Wolfy sprang to her feet and nodded.

"I'm in too," Mum said as she gathered her bandages and stood up.

"Why not?" Sheets added.

Lastly, Z said, "Well, I like this bunch, so what could it hurt?"

When Joe imagined making his confession, he thought it would hurt—and it did. What he did not expect was the immense feeling of a burden lifted. Nor did he expect them to react so strongly. He definitely did not expect a feeling of dedication and commitment to rise up inside of him. It was exhilarating.

"Yes!" Joe said and pounded the table with his fist. "Let's go."

Chins held high, the group walked for the first time as a team, bound together by a goal, propelled by a belief that more might be possible and that they were in this together.

When they arrived at the area of the wall where they had been working, it finally occurred to them that Joe had to pick someone to go first.

Wolfy thought briefly about stepping up, but before she could decide, she heard something that surprised her.

"Okay, I'm going first this time," Joe said.

The team was intrigued.

Joe glanced around at a few clouds, made his selection, and turned to face the team. "Would you please hold these?" he asked Wolfy. Joe handed her his Ray-Bans.

"And can you hold this for me?" he said as he removed his cape and handed it to Sheets, who gladly complied.

Joe stood in front of his chosen cloud. He shook his head clear and ran in place for a few seconds, then closed his eyes and imagined his favorite scares in the past. Then he imagined getting a scare right then and there. He said to himself, "Take a step. Get the scare. Grow. Win." He opened his eyes and took the step.

Joe emerged on the cold tiles in a child's bathroom, the door askew revealing a young, restless boy trying to fall asleep in his bed. The vampire moved swiftly to the side of the bed, grabbed the covers, and ripped them from the boy's body. Joe focused and his eyes caught fire—a green penetrating fire. He hissed and leaned forward, exposing his gleaming white fangs.

The child screamed louder than he'd ever screamed before!

As he came back through and rejoined the team, Joe was greeted like a returning hero.

"For once, I earned it," he thought.

High fives, laughs and smiles, and, thanks to Mum, another tear.

"That was amazing," Sheets said.

Z added, "Seriously, you made that green work!"

"You look bigger," Mum said.

Everyone noticed it. Joe was several inches taller. Scares make monsters grow.

"Thanks. It surprised me a little too," Joe said as he gathered his sunglasses and cape.

The team's mood fell just a bit with his next comment.

"Now it's your turn," Joe said to them.

Before anyone could respond, they saw the smoke trail and heard the sound of the witch approaching. The team's mood darkened.

The witch landed and climbed off of her broom. "I have this morning's reports. Zero scares? Really? You need to throw it into high gear, everyone. You need one hundred scares before the ball tonight. I've seen it done before, so I know it's possible. The committee is waiting for my report, and you know what will happen if you come up short. So, forgive my interruption—now get back to work." She did not take questions. Off she flew.

"Well, that was uplifting," Mum said, breaking the tension.

The entire team laughed as they watched the broom fly away.

"How do we begin?" Joe wondered to himself. He recalled his grandfather's advice to be respectful and help them get that first small win.

"Everyone, listen up," Joe said. "Stop thinking about one hundred scares. Forget it. It's not helpful right now. We need focus. We need to keep it simple. Let's just think about getting one scare for each of us. Just one scare. That's the first step, and every journey proceeds one step at a time. It's your decision—who wants to take the first step?"

"Right here," Wolfy said. "I'm not procrastinating today," she thought. She approached Joe, and to everyone's surprise, she handed him her ears.

Joe smiled and accepted the ears. "You want to know the truth?" he said. "These ears are beautiful, but they don't define you. This task is hard, but you're up to the challenge. It's time to grow. When you're successful, you'll not only grow, but you'll show all of us how it's done. You'll help us take a step toward our goal. You'll help us get closer to being the monsters we were born to be."

Joe's fake enthusiasm was gone. It was replaced by a beautiful sincerity. "Just like me, you're imperfect, yet perfectly capable of becoming your own unique monster."

Wolfy nodded and tried to focus.

The others gathered around, trying not to miss any of it.

"The secret to personal growth is that you're looking for progress, not perfection. You don't have to be the best; you don't have to be proactive all the time. You just have to recognize that sometimes you do have to step up, and for you that time is now. Pick a cloud that works for you."

Wolfy pointed to one and Joe positioned her right in front of it, but still facing him.

"Do me a favor and, just for a moment, close your eyes," he said.

Wolfy closed her eyes.

"Now see yourself being incredibly scary." Joe paused and then said, "Open your eyes. Just go be you. Turn around."

Wolfy turned around to face the cloud.

Joe continued, "Take a step. Get the scare. Grow. Win."

Wolfy stepped forward into the cloud and found herself crouched outside of a child's open bedroom window. She closed her eyes once more and imagined exactly how it should go. She positioned herself to jump, began to snarl loudly, and attracted the attention of the little boy in bed.

The child turned to look and saw a small figure lurking just beyond the window.

Wolfy launched herself through the window and, in midair, began to transform into a frightening werewolf. She landed on the floor next to the bed, bones crackling, hair growing, claws extending.

The child began yelling but he couldn't take his eyes off of the terrifying creature in his room.

Fully transformed, Wolfy stood up on her back legs, drool hanging from the powerful teeth in her mouth, and unleashed a menacing howl.

The child nearly passed out from fear as he dove beneath the covers.

When she emerged, Wolfy was in her normal diminutive body,

but noticeably taller. She was overwhelmed by the moment, shocked by her performance.

"How did that feel?" Joe asked.

"Like I'm fully alive. Like I'm definitely not defective," she replied with pure joy. "I can't believe I did that."

Congratulations flowed as Wolfy composed herself.

Joe surveyed their faces. He could feel it. They were really starting to believe.

"Dear Sheets, please let me share an idea," Joe said, turning toward Sheets. "I realize variety is not your spice, but I hope you'll agree that sometimes new is needed. Sometimes it's worth the risk. It

might even be important for others, not just for you—right?"

"You're going to ask me to take off my mask. I know it," Sheets replied.

Joe continued, "I'm not asking you to try new things all the time. You just have to be open to trying something new once in a while in order to avoid turning unproductive routines into ruts. That's how you build new skills and win. However, it is your call to make."

Sheets looked to Wolfy, shook his head, and thought, "If a vampire with green eyes and a small girl with cat ears can get scares, so can I." He glanced at the team and then repeated the mantra Joe had used with Wolfy: "Take a step. Get the scare. Grow. Win." He removed his mask and asked Mum to hold on to it.

The team looked at his face and worried. Sheets definitely had a very cute baby face. Could it be scary?

Sheets looked thoughtfully at the clouds before him and selected one that felt right. He took the step. He materialized at the foot of the bed of a little girl. She was already stirring, and when Sheets showed up, he immediately caught her eye.

The girl flinched with initial fear and Sheets saw his opening. He stood still, his baby face not moving, other than opening his mouth just a bit to allow a low, "Booooo!" Then he tried something he'd never tried before. He started waving his arms erratically at his sides.

The little girl was clearly scared and used her pillow for a shield.

Emboldened, Sheets reached deeper. He felt powerful, as if he was exploding with light. Looking down, he realized he was in fact exploding with light. His torso was lit up like a blinding disco ball!

"No! Stop!" the girl screamed. And then she was alone.

Sheets walked out of the cloud still baby-faced, but clearly bigger and taller—and he was blushing.

Joe couldn't wait to ask, "How'd that feel?"

"Pretty cool," came the reply.

"And where did those lights come from?" Joe followed up.

"I have no idea. I was just trying something, I guess. I did have an

uncle who could do that, so maybe it
runs in the family," Sheets replied.

Mum handed him his mask, but
for the moment he just held it. He
wasn't ready to cover his face again.

"Okay, Mum," Joe said to his
bandaged teammate. "Are you
willing to give this a shot? I hope
so because I was thinking about
you over lunch. You said others see
you as funny looking. Okay, but
they just don't matter. It feels like
they do sometimes, but they don't.
What matters is how you feel. I was
thinking about Marilyn Monster
with her massive mole. Everyone
loved her 'beauty mark.' I thought
of the famous model Lauren Horror
with that massive gap in her teeth.
She embraced it and made it part of

her signature look. Or what about Mugsy Boos, the shortest basketball player in Monster League history! He learned to use his tiny size to his advantage and once averaged a double-double!"

Joe gently grabbed her by the shoulders. "Your size and your looks and your bandages are not imperfections or flaws. They just are! How you feel about them is your decision. It's up to you to realize they're really your beauty marks."

"Maybe I can do this," Mum thought. What she actually said was, "I'll try, Joe. I want to try." Without missing a beat, she unzipped her hoodie and handed it to Joe. She thoughtfully considered a few clouds and selected one she liked. Quietly, she mumbled, "Take a step. Get the scare. Grow. Win."

When she came through, she was crouching behind a giant teddy bear. Peeking around it, she noticed a kid completely under the covers, using a small flashlight to read a book or comic. She walked in front of the bear and raised her arms in classic mummy fashion.

To get his attention, she kicked one of the bed legs.

The little boy quickly poked his head out to look. His eyes bulged at the sight of Mum approaching him.

Mum fed off this initial reaction, reached into a place she didn't know existed, and released an otherworldly shriek that shook the room!

The kid screamed in response and retreated under the covers.

Mum came through the cloud clearly larger in size, her bandages no longer sagging quite as much.

Joe, Wolfy, and Sheets couldn't contain their glee as they congratulated Mum.

Z, however, started to sweat.

Joe looked his way, but before he could even try to say anything useful, Z started talking.

"I'm too old for this. I ain't got no foot! It's not fair!" the zombie said.

"I have to be honest, Z," Joe said. "You do have certain disadvantages, and they aren't your fault."

"What? I mean, I know!" Z replied, surprised.

"But I have to ask, though," Joe continued. "What is your best choice? I mean, how can you use what you've got instead of fretting over what you don't have? I'm serious—you're smart, right?"

"I am smart," Z acknowledged.

"Then I bet you're smart enough to change how you think about this situation," Joe said. "How can you use what you've got and work around what you don't?" Joe looked at Z's rotting face. "You've got a great face for scaring! That's your power, Z. Own it and use it and I know you'll scare any kid."

Everyone stared at Z.

He nodded approvingly. "Use what I've got," he thought as he used his crutch to hobble toward a cloud.

"It's possible. I just saw the others get it done in style, so maybe I can too," he thought. He found the right cloud but stopped short of walking through. He hung his head and contemplated just quitting.

"Hey, before you go in there, I wanted to give this to you," Joe said. He removed his cape. "I've been thinking about it all morning. I've outgrown it. Another vampire in a cape—we've seen it a million times. You know what I've never seen? A slick zombie in a cape. This will look way better on you if you'll have it."

"It is a beautiful cape. You sure?" Z managed as he accepted the gift.

Joe nodded.

"Hey, Z, hold on one second. I almost forgot," Sheets said and quickly floated away. When he returned a moment later, he held a pair of scruffy, used black Dr. Martens boots. "Mum and I got these at the lost and found while we were on our lunch break. We stuffed the right one with a bunch of newspapers. We figured they might help with walking, and, well, they're cool too."

Z was touched by the show of support. He finished putting on the cape and then carefully laced up his new used boots. He tried a few steps and was amazed at how balanced and stable he felt. After walking around for a minute, he handed Joe his crutch. He smiled at the team and nodded to show appreciation.

"Hey, don't forget—" Joe began to say.

Z held up his hand and grinned. "I know. I know. Take a step. Get the scare. Grow. Win. Got it."

Z walked into the cloud and emerged from the darkness behind a child's open bedroom door. He crinkled up his face and let fly a hideous moaning noise as he approached the child. He was amazed at how quick and secure he felt while walking.

The boy saw that he was about to be overtaken and eaten by a zombie and yelled for help!

Z was so excited! Like Sheets, he found a place inside of himself that he didn't know existed. He decided to try something new. He reached for his jaw and ripped half of it away. It dangled like the rotting limb it was just a few inches from the child.

The poor kid almost passed out from fear.

Z came back larger than all the rest! He snapped his jaw back in place as the team cheered him on.

"Okay, Mr. Z, how did that feel?" Joe asked.

"Definitely not broken. Anything but broken," came the reply and a big smile.

As the team engaged in an animated self-congratulatory conversation, Joe stepped back and watched. He was welling up with emotions. He was happy to have facilitated their progress. He was relieved to have come clean about all of his fears. It was like a fire had been lit. Joe wanted very badly to try again and find out what else was possible.

"I have to say that was pretty amazing. Congratulations, everyone," Joe said. "Now, if you can do that, doesn't it make you curious what else is possible? I'll bet there are a few more things you didn't even know you're capable of. Sometimes, you just don't know until you stretch a little and take a risk."

They all nodded. Joe could see their imaginations working.

Then Wolfy frowned.

"What's wrong?" Joe asked.

"It's amazing what we just did. I'm so happy to be part of this day with this team. But we each just now figured out how to get a scare and the ball is in a few hours. There's no way we can make the quota," Wolfy said.

Everyone sighed.

Magic
Innovation

Joe intentionally stayed quiet as the team slowly began to chat.

"You could be right," Mum said, "but I haven't felt this good . . . ever. So I'm willing to keep trying if you all are."

"I need to keep working and get used to these boots. I'm in," Z said.

"I'm with the zombie!" Sheets said, mask now nowhere to be found.

"Well, then," Wolfy said, "I suppose we have work to do. Does anyone have any ideas?"

Joe watched them start to truly own their decisions, and he wanted to help. "How about we all split up and do our scaring thing, and meet back here in an hour to see where we stand? What do you think?"

Heads nodded and everyone spread out. One by one they selected clouds, went through, and scared the heck out of the little kids on the other side. Wolfy's transformations became faster and faster. Sheets was nearly blinding the children with his amazing lights. Mum actually chose to walk into a room with two sleeping kids and her shriek terrified them both! Z's jaw trick evolved too. At one point he totally removed it and threw it at a child!

An hour later they gathered to compare notes. Their growth, in terms of their talent and physical size, was quite evident. They were really making progress.

"So that's fifty-one scares in all. Good work, to say the least," Joe offered. "Next steps? What do you all think?" Joe again intentionally remained quiet.

"With only a few minutes left, one hundred just isn't possible," Sheets admitted.

"Maybe, but a few hours ago we didn't think getting one scare seemed possible," Mum replied.

"But I like that we're all trying different things," Z said.

"I was thinking the exact same thing!" Joe replied. "When I was talking to the witch, she seemed to understand that all scares aren't created equal."

"What do you mean?" Wolfy asked.

"I mean, if we can produce a small number of truly enormous scares, maybe they will sort of count for more," Joe said. "If we can produce something that blows their mind, maybe they won't care that we didn't reach some arbitrary quota. Maybe they'll realize that what really matters is quality."

"But how?" Mum asked.

"I have an idea I might try," Wolfy said.

"I think I do too," Sheets added.

"I bet they're good ideas, and you know what?" Joe said. "I think we should try some of them together, at the same time."

"Wait. What?" Sheets said.

"Wolfy gave me the idea earlier. She said something about wishing we could go through together. Why can't we?" Joe said.

"That's never been done, has it?" Wolfy asked.

"I've never heard of it," Mum said.

"Me either," Sheets added.

Z looked a little giddy. "But it sounds fun, don't it?"

"Let's work out a possible plan," Joe said and motioned for everyone to gather around.

When they were done, Sheets looked around and found just the right cloud. "Here. This one!"

Sheets, Wolfy, and Joe locked arms and went through together.

This was something that had never been tried before in Monster Land. They emerged from a dark corner of a child's room and Wolfy transformed immediately, her snarls waking the small girl in her bed a few feet away.

The child was clearly shocked and frightened.

Sheets hid behind Wolfy's hulking body and turned on his extravagant light show. The illumination made Wolfy far more menacing.

The child began to cry.

Joe stayed in the dark corner, grabbing stuffed animals and small toys. He threw them randomly over Sheets and Wolfy toward the child just to add to the feeling of complete and total mayhem.

The child ran into her bedroom closet and slammed the door.

"That's a first," Joe thought.

The three monsters emerged from the cloud bigger than ever.

Joe immediately looked at the time. "We've got time for only one more attempt. Are you two ready to go?"

"I saw the perfect cloud, right there," Mum said. "It's a sleepover. Six kids on the floor in a game room."

Mum, Z, and Joe locked arms just like the first team and walked through. They slowly came out of the darkness in the back of the room and launched their plan.

The kids were lying in a tight group near the middle of the room, on the floor, with pillows and blankets everywhere. A television had been left on, giving the room a faint light.

First, Z stomped, surefooted, toward the group. His evil moan gained the kids' attention. Eyes bulged. Behind Z in the dark, Mum let loose with her room-rattling shriek and didn't let up.

Kids started to scream as both sounds combined and blasted their ears.

Using vampire speed and the cover of darkness, Joe zipped around pulling the sheet off of each kid. He tossed all of them in the air and created complete chaos!

One child darted for the door and then the others immediately followed.

"That's a new one too," Joe thought.

The trio smiled and retreated.

Back with the others, they hugged and laughed and slapped hands—knowing they had done their best, knowing they had grown in ways they thought previously unimaginable, knowing that no matter what happened next, they could feel great about their performance.

Then came the familiar sound. They saw the smoke trail. The witch had returned.

"My, my, how big you've all grown, but alas, time is up. Let's see how you did," she said as she glanced at her notes. "Fifty-eight scares in all. That's pretty respectable, but you didn't reach one hundred."

"Maybe so, but we did do a few amazing things," Joe began. "For example, we—"

"I know. I saw it all," she interrupted while pointing to one of several cameras overhead. "And so did the committee. I think you did wonderful. I support the new things you tried. You may have helped all of us rethink what it means to scare. That's how I feel, anyway, but I don't know what the committee will say. They have their ways, and you just shook them up. I'm pulling for you. In any event, well done, monsters.

I hope you enjoy the ball. I'll be in touch soon with the news." As was her practice, she didn't exchange other pleasantries. She hopped on her broom and took off.

The
Monster's
Ball

Outside the dance hall, Joe congratulated the team one more time. "Everyone in Monster Land knows what we did today, for better or for worse. Here's what you helped me figure out. Our fears are somewhat real, but mostly illusions that we allow to persist. Our imperfections are just traits. How we feel about them and use them is up to us. Some of them might even be huge assets. No matter what they say, we won today because we decided to take ownership, be proactive, and to view ourselves in a positive light. I believe this is a skill! It's a habit we're forming. You all have me excited thinking about what else is possible. I can't speak for you, but I don't think any of us are done growing yet. So, I don't care what the committee says, you're all awesome monsters and I'm proud to know you."

"Thanks, Joe," Wolfy said. "You made us a team. You got me moving instead of always hesitating."

"You helped me feel okay about trying new things," Sheets said.

"And you helped me feel cool, strong, and perfectly imperfect," Mum chimed in.

"Dude, you called me out on the excuses. I needed it. I owe you," Z said.

Joe's green eyes got just a little misty. As they shared their kind words, Joe silently thought of his grandfather and thanked him for the inspiration.

"You all taught me to lead better than any training program probably ever could," Joe said in response. "You ready to do this? Keep in mind there might be a few jealous looks—I mean, you are all ginormous!"

"Wait. What does your shirt mean?" Wolfy asked.

Joe was dressed uncharacteristically casual in a white T-shirt with the letters S S G W scrawled in handwritten black letters.

He smiled while he pointed to each letter and said, "Take a step. Get the scare. Grow. Win. It feels kind of like our new motto."

The team responded with affirming nods and then walked through the big doors and into the ballroom. Most of the other monsters were in awe. First, the team was huge! Second, they looked so amazing.

Joe was wearing his beloved shades, but he wasn't hiding. They were just cool. His eyes were like an emerald fire, casting shards of green light out from behind the lenses.

Sheets still wasn't wearing a mask. He glided in with a big grin on his baby face, and a cacophony of lights exploding from his body.

Wolfy entered transformed as a massive, scary werewolf, and also totally cute with little cat ears on top of her head.

Mum left the hoodie behind for once, proud of her perfectly fitting bandages. She added a few long, elegant scarves around her neck to complete the look.

Z donned the cape and the always cool boots. He added a top hat to the ensemble that worked perfectly. He was the most dapper zombie in the place.

"We're at a monster's ball. Shall we go show them how it's done?" Wolfy asked.

Quickly, Wolfy, Sheets, Mum, and Z hit the dance floor and started grooving.

Joe stood there for a moment and watched with no small amount of pride and joy. He wished his grandfather could have been there to see it.

The witch approached and looked up at Joe. "I'm a fan now. You did something special today. The administration is impressed, too, from what I heard, but they won't have their official decision for the group until later. So, what have you learned from all of this?"

Joe didn't hesitate. "That all monsters are beautiful, valuable, and so very capable. I realized that imperfections can be strengths and misfits can make magic. I also learned that while one monster who believes is formidable, a monster squad is unstoppable."

What she said next surprised him.

"Joe, I'm here to offer you a job. They want you. They think you'd be

a great addition to the committee.
It's not official yet, and like I said,
I honestly don't know what they'll
decide about the others, but you—
they want you on their team. What
do you say?"

"With respect, I have to decline.
I think I belong in the field. What
could be better than working with
a team like that?" he said as he
pointed to his gyrating monster
friends on the dance floor.

The witch replied, "But what will
I tell the committee?"

Joe grabbed his phone, hit a
button to record a video, and flipped
the screen to shoot himself. He
pushed his shades to the top of his
head to reveal his potent green eyes.

"Hi, committee. Joe Vampire here. On behalf of my team, I'd like to thank you for the opportunity to prove ourselves. If you love what we did, well, you're welcome. If you're not sure about our tactics, apologies, but I know you like those results, right? I greatly appreciate your offer to join the committee, but I don't think that role fits me. I'd like to stay out here in the field and help a few more monsters grow. If you grant me continued monster status, that would be spectacular, but unless my team also receives the same treatment, I will have to voluntarily turn in my monster card. You know, in a short period of time, we really made some strides. We tried, we failed, we tried again, and we created some of the best scares anyone has ever seen. Along the way I realized that each one of us is somehow defective, weak, and broken, but that's beautiful in its own way—and we're still perfectly capable of creating amazing work. That's the joy of being a monster. Our flaws don't limit us. They define our uniqueness. Thanks for helping us figure this out. Sincerely—the monster squad."

Joe sent the video to the witch and headed out to the dance floor. "I wonder what my father will think when he finds out I turned down a spot on the committee," Joe thought. "Who cares! I know where I belong. Right here—dancing with monsters."

PART
3

The Decision

S o, I should start wearing Ray-Bans to work?" Noah asked as they both finished reading the story.

Maria playfully hit him once again. "No! The story is about many things, but one of the main points is about facing your fears."

"I know. I know," Noah said. "The whole team did, then at the end Joe took a huge risk. He gave the committee an ultimatum. I bet that level of pure candor and authenticity feels amazing, but it sure would be risky in real life."

"You don't have to give an ultimatum for them to get rid of Miles or move

Miles or anything," Maria explained. "But you do need to be confident going into the new role."

"Joe didn't accept the role," Noah said.

"He didn't want it, but you do," Maria replied. "Joe was chasing a great fit, just like you."

"You're right. You are always better at thinking through these things," Noah admitted.

Maria smiled warmly.

"I've got it now. I think I know the solution," Noah said.

"Tell me," she said.

"You gave it to me, sort of. You and Joe," he began. "I will accept the role as long as I know that I have the latitude to manage my team as I see fit. I will apply an honest but respectful version of the three strikes approach for dealing with Miles and then act accordingly. Do you remember the three strikes rule from that same professor?" he asked.

"Sure. One mistake or slight is just an incident. Don't overreact. Two mistakes or slights might require a more forceful response, but nothing severe. Don't assume the worst about the person. If there's a third incident, that's a clear pattern—three strikes and you're out. Time to deliver far more concrete consequences. I think it was something like that."

"You nailed it," Noah said. "So, I need to calm down. Firing him needs clear and compelling documentation and may or may not happen later. I'll manage him as he needs to be managed, gradually increasing the consequences. Over time that might mean using a coach, a formal reprimand, a role change, or letting him go. If I build a clear case while helping the team improve, I need to know they will back me."

"So, you're going to accept the offer, but talk to them about your needs as the leader of the group?" Maria summarized.

"Yes, and I won't even have to name names. They will know exactly what I'm talking about. I'll make it very clear that I'm thrilled to accept the offer, but I do expect to be able to manage performance issues as I see fit. I'll tell them my goal is peace and productivity and I'll do what it takes to achieve them." Noah took a deep breath and smiled. "That feels right. I'm excited."

"So, aside from dealing with Miles, what will you do to help the team?" she asked.

"My working theory is that most of their dysfunction is due to Miles. When they see me proactively addressing him, that alone should improve things. Plus, the leader who is leaving—the person I'm replacing— was well known to be, well, aloof. You know, the type of boss who doesn't interact with the team much and is quick to point out problems that were mostly caused by unclear expectations. I'll work hard to be more clear, more available, and more helpful. I want to actually get to know the team."

"That sounds like an amazing plan, Mr. Manager," Maria said as she stood up. She gave him a little kiss and sat back down. "I'm so proud of you, and I'm so happy we met back in school."

Noah noticed that Maria immediately started using her tablet. "What are you doing?"

"Finding a good restaurant! Tonight, we are celebrating you, babe," she said.

Noah immediately started playing on his phone.

"Are you telling your boss about your decision?" she asked.

"Nope. I'm telling Dad we need to talk. I've got to explain this to him before he hears something from his buddy," Noah replied.

"Well, then, there is only one last issue," Maria said.

"What's that?" Noah replied.

"Choosing what to be for Halloween. I've gotta go with the ghost! Look at my baby face!"

"Then I'm Joe Vampire," Noah replied excitedly. "I'll even wear the Ray-Bans."

"You should drop our old professor a note," Maria said. "I wonder if he's still around. Anyway, he'd love to hear about how the book made a difference."

"Good idea," Noah replied. He opened his laptop, head spinning with a rapidly growing list of things to do. He felt a rush of joy. "I don't know where this decision will take me," he thought, "but I do know it's time for me to go dancing with monsters."

DISCUSSION

N oah was able to make a huge
decision because he chose
to dance with his monsters. Joe
became a good leader because
he learned to dance with his
monsters. Wolfy, Sheets, Mum,
and Z all learned to be successful
because they chose to dance with
their monsters. They all overcame
their fears and successfully
claimed a better version of
themselves.

It's important to remember
that we all experience a variety of

difficult thoughts and feelings. We have fears, apprehensions, worries, anxieties, and so on. Sometimes they are functional. Mostly they slow us down and cause problems. The most important thing that you need to hear about this reality is that you are normal!

To begin claiming your better self, sometimes you have to get over yourself, stop making excuses, and find the courage to step forward. It starts with a little self-reflection and honesty. So, what is it you fear? What is your monster? What are you going to do about it? Will you take a step as Joe encouraged?

Let's slow down for a minute and think about these questions.

What Do You Fear?

You fear that something bad is possible or likely. That might include mistakes or failure, looking incompetent, being judged, being harmed, experiencing disapproval, being flawed and not worthy, and so on. All humans experience fear, and all humans are flawed. For most of us, these issues are always present and sometimes cause damage.

Why Do You Fear?

You fear things for many reasons. You might be born more likely to experience certain fears. Your parents may have made you fearful of certain things, intentionally or not. Friends, teachers, neighbors, and many others may have contributed as well. No matter the origin, fear is everywhere—it's common.

Your Fears Make You Do Unproductive Things.

The more you feel the weight of your fears and imperfections (real or perceived), the more you question yourself. Several particularly thorny tendencies often emerge. They make socializing, decision-making, and creating good work more difficult. Common examples include:

Blaming Others

It's a natural reaction to many situations. Blame the situation, your

resources, your colleagues, your
boss, your employees, your client,
your parents, your education, your
zip code, and so on. Sometimes the
object of your blame does provide
a partial explanation for whatever
outcome is bothering you. However,
blame rarely helps. Mostly, it stops
you from examining yourself and
moving forward. Admit that blame
isn't useful, own things to the best of
your ability, and move on.

Becoming Closed off and Reluctant to Try New Things

When fear clouds your mind, *new*
often becomes equated with *risky*.
If you're lacking confidence, feeling
blue, or dealing with a recent

setback, risk sounds horrible. This is when unproductive routines become deeply ingrained ruts. Given that change is the only constant, you're increasingly ill-prepared for what's next. Growth stops. A downward spiral becomes possible.

Procrastinating

Procrastination is the art of convincing yourself that now is not necessary. It's a choice that often requires great energy and creativity in the face of evidence that action is needed immediately. It, too, can become a habit, a rut, a typical first response. While no one is ever completely free of this tendency, we do know that successful people resist it strongly.

Developing a Negative Self-Image

This may be the most damaging
tendency since it influences
everything else. A negative self-
image pushes you to assign
yourself as the object of blame, to
become more risk averse, and to
procrastinate even more. It kills
your confidence. It is the negative
mental glue that slows you down in
so many different ways.

You Can Overcome Your Fears.

For some people, fears and
apprehensions can be put in check.
They cease to be big obstacles.
For a smaller group of people,
they can actually become assets.
Fears become opportunities to
grow. Flaws are understood to be

unique traits—assets to be loved and leveraged.

Living mostly unencumbered by fear is achieved when negative thoughts, feelings, and behaviors are overshadowed by stronger positive thoughts, feelings, and behaviors. More specifically:

Ownership > Blaming

You must openly accept responsibility for yourself and admit that—external factors aside— you are in charge of what happens to you. Blaming feels momentarily justified and satisfying but rarely helps. Indulging blame can lead to less-than-optimal decisions about how to move forward. It reinforces a negative mentality. You want to understand constraints but stop short of blaming. The best course is to choose to honestly own your role in the situation and then make great choices while respecting but not fearing any constraints you face.

Open-Mindedness > Reluctance

You will need to try new things, at least sometimes. You will come to see that change is what you make of it, and that making change can be fun. None of us are perfectly open-minded. We all have many odd filters and feelings built in that make us like some things and resist others. Just know that growth and success will require you to improve how much you allow yourself to be open to new ideas, new ways of doing things, new people, and so on. Reluctance isn't wrong. It's natural, and sometimes can keep you safe, but if growth is your goal, it can never be as strong as openness.

Proactivity > Procrastination

You have to believe in the power of now. Actively try to sense the danger in putting things off. Realize that to procrastinate is to choose to be less productive. Ultimately, it will make you feel worse about yourself. It will also send a negative signal about you to others. On the other hand, proactivity not only improves productivity, but it also accelerates learning. Thankfully, with practice, being proactive can become a habit. The best part is that when you embrace being proactive, you get to experience the joy of getting things done more quickly.

Value of Uniqueness > Weight of Imperfections

You must realize your flaws and imperfections are just expressions of your originality. They define you, but you get to write the definitions. Your height, body type, facial features, and eye color; the sound of your voice, how you walk, your mannerisms; your interests, preferences, and tendencies. They are all basically good, but then others somehow convince you they are imperfections. Once you realize that you always were and still remain unique and valuable, you discover the power to write the definitions yourself.

————

Note that each of these ideas is expressed in equation form. This is just a reminder that the more difficult or less useful side of the equation never really goes away completely, but you can keep these tendencies in check through self-awareness and action. Stated differently, you're beautifully imperfect—so what? You're choosing progress over perfection. Just work hard to tip the scales toward the more productive side of the equation. That's progress and it is within your grasp! Perfection is an impossible goal that will crush anyone.

Practical Advice for Overcoming Your Fears

There are many behaviors and activities that will help you tip the equations in the right direction. Here are a few of the best ones:

Identifying False Constraints

Your fears lead to beliefs about the constraints you will face moving forward. Like fears, some constraints are more real than others. You spend so much time and energy worrying about constraints that don't exist, or on constraints that aren't as big as you imagined. When you think about a task, project, relationship, or goal, don't assume you fully understand the constraints you face. Whether it's a resource, person, time, or some other constraint, remember to test your thoughts. Can you understand the constraint differently? Can someone else help you reimagine it as not so troublesome? Can certain preemptive actions help you reduce or remove the constraint? The more you study and break down the constraints you perceive, the more you understand their real nature and what you can do to overcome them.

Trying New Things

Facing your fears, in part, is about bravery. Bravery isn't just a baseline trait you're born with; it's a learned ability to face challenges and uncertainties. That's why stretching yourself, at work and outside of work, is so important. You are not trying to become addicted to variety. You just want to find decent comfort with the unknown. You need not travel the globe or otherwise spend money to achieve this feat. Just think about what you eat (and when and with whom), the movies you enjoy, how you spend your leisure dollars, the route you take for your daily walk, and so on. Mix them up—at least a little. This shakes up the brain and increases higher level thinking. The secondary benefits of this behavior include more creativity and better memory. The primary benefit is an increased comfort with discomfort! That gives

you more guts when needed to face
your fears and succeed.

Building a Support Team

No matter how strong you might be,
you'll overcome your fears faster
when your team is strong too. A
good team helps you believe you can
overcome anything. They provide
perspective and suggestions. They
help you get back on track when
needed. Overall, they amplify all of
the strengths you bring to the task.
Your team needs to know the fear
you're pondering. They need to know
how you feel about it, what you want
to do about it, and how they might
be helpful. They have your back and
will work to make sure you don't
fall when you begin to engage. From

advice to kindness to actual helping hands, a good team will make your task far easier.

Choosing Perspective

Perspective refers to how you choose to think about an object (e.g., an issue, person, situation). It's a choice. Too often it's a subconscious choice driven by habit. If you're interested in facing your fears and embracing success, you're going to break that habit and make it a conscious choice you engage regularly. Is the object a threat or an opportunity? Is it defeating or uplifting? Is it a burden to carry or a chance to learn and grow? Is it confounding or a fun puzzle to solve? The answers to these questions are partially

driven by objective reality and
also meaningfully influenced by
how you choose to view the issue.
It is not always easy. You will not
always be successful in redefining
an object in your mind. However,
most of the time it works, and it
gives you an edge. Find the positive
perspective when you think about
your fears. There are many to choose
from: using positive imagery to see
yourself getting past this issue,
recalling similar situations in
the past and how you successfully
managed them, thinking about the
worst thing that can happen and
then seeing yourself growing past it,
understanding that you're not alone
and others have faced the same
fear, and so on. Now you're building

the habit of choosing perspectives
capable of helping you move past
your fears.

Asking for Help

One of the risks associated with
facing your fears and improving
yourself is that you run into difficult
moments that make you want to
quit. When you chase a goal, you
have volunteered to try hard, take
risks, and fight through the fear.
Great, but that process sometimes
results in moments where you feel
at your limit or even broken. This is
normal and you can survive these
moments. The key is to think about
how you're feeling daily, so you are
aware when these moments are
approaching. Engage in meaningful

self-care, and if needed, be brave and seek the additional help you need. That might be a member of your support team, a coach, a mentor, or an appropriate mental health professional. Think of it this way—we all need a little assistance once in a while, and if you haven't felt the need to ask for help in a long time, you're clearly not getting close enough to your limits! Push hard, but when life is too much, be wise and ask for help.

Good Leaders Help People with This Journey.

Your employees are not human resources. They are people. They have personalities, needs, and problems that you don't fully understand. You don't know them as well as you think you do. They are human, just like you, and deserve all of the kindness and respect you deserve.

Sure, sometimes you might need to speak frankly to address performance issues or questionable behaviors. But if you want to keep them engaged and committed to the team, you have to be thoughtful, not just clear, when communicating. Helping the team reach goals is just part of a leader's work. You have to move past only thinking about performance to also work on developing others and supporting employee well-being as central to your long-term success.

Truly effective leaders help people grow, belong, and feel heard. Having the people skills needed to make this happen is more important than IQ or any amount of subject matter expertise. Good relationships move employees past minimal compliance to feel real commitment. They create a feeling of purpose beyond a paycheck. They turn a group of people into a team.

There are many behaviors that help leaders create productive teams. A few in particular represent very important rules to remember:

Collaborate, Don't Dictate

This encompasses inclusion, voice, and transparency. You might have authority, but you shouldn't always

use it when making decisions. No
adult truly enjoys being told what
to do or enjoys being excluded from
a decision that affects them. Even
when you do need to use simple
authority sometimes, it should be
transparent and clearly explained.
If your goal is great decisions, you
want the team's input. If you want
them invested and committed, you
need to give them real ownership.
Some decisions should only be
made by you. Most should be
collaborative discussions owned
somewhat equally. Some can be
owned by the team with little input
from you. When in doubt and when
time allows, lean toward more
collaboration and inclusion. Genuine
inclusion in decision-making

validates their expertise, shows that you are a fair facilitator, and significantly increases how strongly they own the final decision. To adopt this approach, you will have to learn to get over yourself. Leadership is mostly about them, not you.

Candor, Not Just Kindness

While positivity is absolutely vital, being candid is even more essential for sustained performance. You often hear about the importance of being positive. What you don't hear is that pure kindness and positivity won't optimize relationships or performance all by themselves. Thankfully, the liberal use of kindness and positivity provides the needed context within which candor becomes very useful. Candor means straight talk, no unnecessary innuendo, and no beating around the bush. Real, sometimes difficult, information and thoughts that need to be shared. Candor is often needed; however, to understand how it might be received, context matters a lot. In toxic workplaces, candor won't help anyone. It just makes things worse. In workplaces defined by kindness and positivity, candor is useful and clarifying and becomes quite digestible and practical. Civility is lovely, but candor must be strong too. It is worth noting that you have crossed a line if candor hurts or creates fear. Fear and negativity are never good choices when trying to motivate a team. They may bring short-term compliance, but almost always weaken long-term commitment.

Opportunities, Not Obstacles

Perspective is not only a tool you use when learning to overcome your fears. It's a powerful tool for leaders as well. The way you choose to think about an issue, then how you craft a message about the issue, and how you deliver that message can be transformational. If a key customer requires something special and you and the team need to work over the weekend, how they feel about it depends a lot on how the issue is framed (not just the incentives you may or may not offer). Is this just an unexpected task, something

you're so sorry you have to ask
for, and a thing to be loathed? Or
is this a chance to win a little job
security and goodwill by helping an
important customer who's in a bind?
Assuming you have a little goodwill
with the team and assuming this
doesn't happen too often, you can
shape a challenging issue to make a
positive impression. So, is the glass
empty, half full, or overflowing?
That's your call. Remember,
perspective is everything.

Authenticity, Not Acting

Few of you were trained to act,
but most of you go to work every
day and act a lot anyway. You
manage impressions to meet the
expectations of your supervisor,

employees, peers, clients, vendors, and so on. This is a sign of social intelligence. It's also a behavior that is completely overindulged. So much so that most professional relationships feel oddly contrived, distant, and transactional. The most successful leaders replace a good amount of impression management with authenticity. That just refers to a version of you that is a bit more honest, less filtered, and more forthright. It applies to how you look, how you treat others, and how you speak about all of the issues at work. Even when they don't like something about you or your view on an issue, they almost always appreciate authenticity. So be a little more vulnerable and open, own your views, laugh at yourself, and share a story that humbles and humanizes you once in a while. When done correctly, being vulnerable and showing your humanity will not erode others' confidence in you. It just makes you more approachable while validating their humanity at the same time. In the end, authenticity is easier than acting, and it often evokes authenticity from others. That's the beginning of real rapport and trust.

Be the Change, Not the Boss

Actions do speak louder than words, so remember that your best motivational tool is always to model the way. To model the way just means to walk the talk. Even more to the point, do a little less talking and a little more showing. If you say you believe in hard work, they should see you working very hard. If you say you believe in inclusion, they need to see you bringing people into the conversation. If you say you believe in creativity, they must see you showing sincere interest when new ideas arise. Humans learn through observation quite well because it's a low-risk opportunity to learn. From a motivational perspective, remember that employees are driven by compensation (but not nearly as much as you might think) and by how much they feel purpose in their work. However, the biggest explanation for their motivation is the quality of the relationships

they engage in every day, and
none is more impactful than
their relationship with you—their
supervisor. You do live in a glass
house—and they are watching—so be
mindful of your behaviors!

———————

There are of course another
hundred ideas you should consider.
For example, the story noted
progress, not perfection. That is a
great reminder for anyone feeling
overwhelmed by the size of the
task in front of them. Or how about
the need to connect to purpose?
Can you show the team why their
work really matters? Or one of my
favorites: manage outcomes, not
process. Use autonomy to show
them respect and get involved only

when the work produced does not meet expectations, as opposed to micromanaging. One size does not fit all is another classic alluded to in the story. We are all wonderfully different, requiring leaders to tailor their efforts. Another essential that is becoming truer every year is maintaining a learning orientation. For you and the team, be aware of how fast knowledge decays and of the need to refresh your skills. The list of useful ideas is long and interesting, but those noted above provide an amazing place to start.

People Drive Innovation.

The first step toward success, for any individual or leader, is overcoming fears and learning to communicate at a deeper level. When people on a team are all engaging this process in their own way (hopefully facilitated by a competent supervisor), this creates understanding and trust. This is the interpersonal foundation required for next-level conversations. People feel more comfortable and motivated to speak up, to respectfully disagree and debate. This empowerment dynamic is the pool from which creative ideas emerge. Then innovation is about the team figuring out how to get real value out of creative ideas. However, it all begins with a team that experiences enough psychological safety to feel comfortable engaging in thought, conversations, and behaviors beyond the minimum requirements. From this perspective, it becomes so clear why authenticity, kindness, vulnerability, humility, and related notions are so inextricably linked to creativity and innovation.

Empathy Kick-Starts All of This!

To effectively lead others, you must know and like yourself. You must engage a meaningful amount of self-love and self-care. To help others with personal growth in your role as a leader, you must care for them too. To really connect, you must feel and understand what they are going through (at least partially)—that's empathy. When you show real empathy, people know it, and only

then can they start to believe in
you. From a leadership perspective,
this tells the team they are part
of a positive human relationship,
not just a simple transaction.
That's when employees become far
more likely to try and achieve for
themselves, the team, and for you.
Empathy kick-starts the process of
everyone learning to understand and
appreciate each other. It allows deep,
respectful relationships to emerge.

A General Process
for Improvement

Get over yourself. Joe learned
to get over himself and began to
understand empathy. The next thing
you know, he's embracing "take a

step, get the scare, grow, win" and sharing it with the team. Let's break that down.

Take a Step

You could start by talking about defining your goal. You have to set your sights on something before you can go get it: a task for the day, a goal for the month or year, a dream for your career. However, my experience is that most people can define their targets fairly easily. It's the getting started part where they need help. Take a step means to get started. Move, try, engage. You'll learn and improve as you go, but all of your aspirations are just illusions if you don't get up and begin walking toward them.

Get the Scare

This is about doing the work needed to be successful. After the first step, there is a second and a third. You must dive in and be persistent. The people with the most intelligence sometimes win, but not as often as you'd imagine. Most successful people are better defined as hardworking and resilient, regardless of intelligence or other potential advantages they might have. They keep working when others tire, and they make personal sacrifices as needed. They take the punches, get back up, and keep moving. They understand the question "How bad do you want it?"

Grow

This part is about rapid learning during the course of chasing a task or goal. I'm not referring to long-term investments in courses, degrees, or other educational endeavors. I'm talking about short-term reflection on your performance and how it might change and improve. This means honest analysis of available performance data, self-reflection about your thoughts and behaviors, and the pursuit of feedback from relevant others (e.g., colleagues, clients, your supervisor, a coach). Get honest about how you're doing, sooner rather than later. Make needed adjustments and keep moving forward.

Win

You achieved something. Now what? This is a reminder that even though a journey defined by self-improvement and helping others is a giant reward in and of itself, we do need to stop and celebrate ourselves from time to time. You definitely want to stop and smell the roses when you reach certain plateaus. Whether you're focusing only on yourself or an entire team, you need to recognize the big moments, insights, and wins achieved. Enjoy the feeling of growth and accomplishment—it's sweet! Then smile and acknowledge that more is still possible and begin the process again.

A Note about "Fit" and Your Career

Fit is probably my favorite career topic. Fit refers to how well who you are meshes with what you do. It's about the match between your personality, skills, and interests and the demands of the job. Some people barely tolerate their work. They feel they have no other choices or maybe they feel locked into their current role due to income or other things that are hard to give up. Most people are a mix of enjoying what they do, merely tolerating their work, and hating what they do. Sadly, many others dislike what they do full-time, but again, feel somehow locked into their current situation.

The dream is a strong fit. With a strong fit you don't dread the boss, you don't feel weird on Sundays knowing Monday is right around the corner, and challenges generally feel like fun puzzles. Completed work is fulfilling, not just a relief. You gain pleasure from your work regularly. Most of the time you are able to focus, stay productive, and be creative—all while feeling positive!

To be clear, fit and passion are not the same but are related. Fit gives you a high baseline level of fulfillment and positivity. Passion is a serious feeling of excitement or enthusiasm directed at an object, such as your job or a task at work. It waxes and wanes for a variety of reasons, but on average, the experience of passion will be more frequent when fit is high.

I am not naïve. I know that everyone cannot love what they do. Everyone cannot experience high fit. I also know that far too few people experience high fit because they are afraid to go find it! The journey to find it isn't risk free. As was the case with Noah and Joe, it's up to you to decide how much risk you're willing to endure to get the thing you want.

Let me help you start thinking about your journey by offering a simple framework.

Step one is to define a path. Stated differently, before initiating

any kind of career change, you
have to have a clear destination
as your target. Depending on your
age and career stage, your effort
might include reading books and
blogs, watching educational videos,
taking courses, reading relevant
news, looking up salaries and other
statistics, networking with people
who can enlighten you, and so on.
Through knowledge you can make a
smart choice about how you might
shift or completely transform
your career.

Next, with an actual target in
sight, do the homework. What
will it take to get there? You must
understand the specific skills
you will need to be minimally
qualified for your desired role.

You also might need one or more specific new credentials to signal your competence and readiness. Prepare to find and possibly pay for the resources and tools you need to make the change happen (e.g., a recruiter, a coach, a premium LinkedIn account). Finally, brush up on your networking skills and hone your elevator pitch.

The only thing left to do is to follow Joe's advice and take a step!

Questions to Consider

1. When the group members first started sharing about themselves, Joe did not. This is common. Why do leaders hesitate to be vulnerable?

Should they be more
vulnerable?

2. It would have been justified
to just remove the group from
field activities given their
performance. Was the decision
to give them one unique last
chance smart or not?

3. Thanks to a lack of
confidence, the team indulges
unproductive behaviors
that include blaming others,
procrastination, being
closed off and not open to
new things, and having a
negative self-image. Have
you ever been challenged by
these tendencies?

4. Z in particular likes to make
excuses. They were his crutch.

Have you ever over-relied on a particular excuse?

5. Have you ever been assigned a goal that you thought was impossible? What happened? Can really difficult goals be useful?

6. What do the clouds represent?

7. Each of the monsters' initial attempts failed. What are the main leadership rules Joe violated when talking to each of them individually before they stepped into the cloud? (For example: collaborate, don't dictate.)

8. After the early failures, Joe spent time alone in self-reflection. He got honest about himself and the team. It helped

him define a path forward. Have you ever experienced something like this?

9. Joe engaged the team with humility, authenticity, and even self-deprecation. Have you, or someone you observed, ever engaged others in this manner? How did it go?

10. Joe worries about how his family views him. He worries about how strangers view him too. Can you relate to this? Why do we do this? Is it a good thing?

11. When they arrived at the wall a second time, Joe went first. Why was this useful?

12. Have you seen Joe's small-wins approach (i.e., just get one scare) work in your career?

13. Creating a performance breakthrough isn't just about individual effort. It's about the team. For example, the team helped Z get his first scare. The team later worked together to create several truly huge scares. Can you think of a time you, or someone you observed, got a needed boost from the team? What did the team do?

14. Joe developed empathy for the team. The team eventually had empathy for Joe. Members of the team had empathy for each other. Sometimes we struggle to feel empathy. Why? How can you help yourself or others experience empathy?

15. Some say necessity is the mother of invention. Do you think the team would have tried the interesting things they tried if it were just a normal workday, and they were not in jeopardy of losing their monster status? What are the implications of your answer for the typical leader at work?

16. Do you agree with Noah's decision? What do you think about speaking candidly to your supervisor about your needs and expectations?

17. Joe and Noah are both seeking a stronger fit in their careers. Do you have a great fit? What specific things do you need to

do to achieve a better fit over
the next several years?

18. What is your biggest fear?
When did it start? What
impact has it had on you?

19. For the most important
challenge or goal you currently
face, what is the step you
need to take and why are you
hesitating?

20. Are Ray-Bans and Dr. Martens
really that cool? Yes. Yes,
they are.

ACKNOWLEDGMENTS

Writing this book was a joy. However, the path to publishing *Dancing with Monsters* was unexpected. I had finished the first draft and was thinking about publishing the book myself when I received a note from Dean Karrel. Dean is one of the great course authors at LinkedIn Learning. Since we are both in that wonderful library of courses, we'd become friends and had been following each other for a number of years. One day, when Dean found himself unable to accept a particular speaking opportunity, he thought of me. He knew who I was as an author and speaker and was kind enough to connect me with Laura Gachko. Laura was looking for someone to deliver a keynote at an event for the Audio Publishers Association. She booked me for what turned out to be a great event and in one of our conversations, she asked me, "Do you know Matt Holt?" I said I did not. She connected us. The rest is history. Thank you, Dean. Thank you, Laura.

When I met Matt, I was immediately taken by his candor. It was very refreshing. When we agreed to work together, he promised he would be supportive and hands off—and he was. Matt,

I really value your honesty and straight talk. To the entire team at Matt Holt Books (part of BenBella Books)—especially Katie Dickman— thank you for helping to shape and polish this project. You nudged a little here and there and the book is clearly better for it.

To my wife, Cheryl, thanks for the never-ending support and assistance. Cheryl is always my first reader. She tells it like it is and doesn't sugarcoat anything. When she told me she really loved this book, that was a first—and I knew I was on to something. She continues to help me with this project in many ways, all while dealing with chemotherapy and all of the fun that comes with cancer. You are such a survivor. Thanks for everything.

Thanks also to my son Paxon Dewett and my dear friend Laura Dewett who also served as early sources of feedback. Your comments were very useful and appreciated.

Last but not least, to all of the educators I have known throughout my life who helped me believe that it's okay to try and fail—thank you! The learning derived from this predictable process drives personal change and improvement. This book is a good example. Before it was a pretty good fable, it was a really bad novel! Thanks to writing the wrong book, I could more clearly see the right book.

ABOUT THE AUTHOR

Dr. Todd Dewett is a globally recognized leadership educator, author, and speaker. After working with Andersen Consulting and Ernst & Young, he completed his PhD at Texas A&M University in Organizational Behavior and enjoyed ten years as an award-winning professor at Wright State University. He's delivered over 1,000 speeches around the world and created a library of online courses enjoyed by millions of professionals. His clients include Microsoft, IBM, GE, Ernst & Young, State Farm, Kraft Heinz, Boeing, MD Anderson, ExxonMobil, and hundreds more. Visit his home online at www.drdewett.com.

Dr. Dewett delivers inspiring keynotes!

Book Todd for your event:

https://www.drdewett.com/book-todd/

Join thousands of companies
and millions of learners who love
Dr. Dewett's library of leadership
and career-related courses at
LinkedIn Learning:

https://www.linkedin.com/learning
/instructors/todd-dewett

For all other inquiries:

www.drdewett.com